BAPTISM

Moreno Dal Bello

B A P T I S M

Baptism, as taught by the Roman Catholic Church, is *the Sacrament of spiritual rebirth by which one becomes 'born-again' and cleansed from all sins.* This Roman Catholic teaching is in contradiction with the Roman Catholic Bible, which shows that Baptism was **never** administered to **make** a person a true believer, but was **always** something that was performed on those who were **already** born-again believers. The concept of baptismal regeneration, along with many other Roman Catholic teachings such as the Rosary and Purgatory, does not originate from within the Roman Catholic Church, but emanates from the bowels of Paganism.

WHAT IS BAPTISM? –
 THE ROMAN CATHOLIC VIEW

Baptism, according to the Church of Rome, is the first of seven Sacraments. The Roman Catholic Catechism teaches that a Sacrament is *"...an external sign or action chosen by Christ to give grace."*[1]

The Roman Catholic Church teaches, in total contrast with her own Bible, that Baptism *"Cleanses us from original sin by giving sanctifying grace, and so we become the children of God, and members of Christ's Mystical Body, the Church."[2]*

Vatican II reaffirmed this teaching by insisting that *"By the sacrament of Baptism man becomes truly incorporated into the crucified and glorified Christ, and is reborn to a sharing of the divine life."[3]*

Romanism's baptismal rites are performed upon infants as soon as possible after birth, for Roman Catholics are taught to believe that the soul which is not baptized is eternally lost. Baptism in the Roman Catholic Church is administered by the priest, who sprinkles 'holy' water on the head of the infant whilst saying, *'I baptize thee in the name of the Father, and of the Son, and of the Holy Ghost.'*

So absolutely vital is this sacrament that, according to Rome, one cannot enter heaven without it. However, there are two exceptions to this rule, as Roman Catholic **Bishop Hay** explains. The first is: *"The case of an infidel converted in a heathen land, where it is impossible to get baptism"*; and the second: *"The case of a martyr 'baptized' as it is called, 'in his own blood'; but in all other cases, whether of young or old, the necessity is 'absolute.'"[4]* It is also the teaching of Romanism that an act of perfect love toward God can replace the sacrament of baptism.

The Trent Catechism states the following: *"Infants, unless regenerated unto God through the grace of baptism, whether their parents be Christian or infidel, are born to eternal misery and perdition."* This doctrine was so horrific, that a 'better place' needed inventing for infants who died without baptism. *Limbus Infantum* is its name; Roman Catholics know it as 'Limbo'.

This is truly one of the most oppressive, non-biblical doctrines to have come out of the Roman Catholic Church. Roman Catholic Catechisms now inform followers that, *"Infants who die without baptism go to a place of happiness (Limbo), BUT THEY WILL NEVER SEE GOD IN HEAVEN!"*[5] Adding to the grief of the parents, the dead unbaptized child is even refused burial by a Roman Catholic priest in 'consecrated' ground.

"The primary purpose of the Church of Rome in excluding unbaptized infants from heaven is to force parents to commit their children to her as soon as possible. The long range design is to bring all people into subjection to her, to put her stamp of ownership on every person possible. And the pressure put on Roman Catholic parents to see to it that their children are baptized early is almost unbelievable—a commitment which once she receives she never relinquishes."[6]

It is baptism into the Roman Catholic Church, rather than salvation by grace through faith in Jesus Christ, alone, that is taught by Romanism as the means to salvation. It is the effects of the sacrament of water baptism that the Roman Catholic Church speaks of when she talks of being 'born again', or 'born from above'. Baptism is also commonly referred to by Roman Catholics as the 'second birth'.

Roman Catholicism contends that, in baptism, a miracle is performed by the priest who 'charges' the water with the grace of God. *"Their phrase is that they work 'ex opere operato'. In other words, it is no longer just water, it is charged with the grace of God, and therefore when it is put upon that child a miracle is worked in the child."*[7]

However, as with all the Roman Catholic sacraments, doubt is placed upon the absolute certainty of baptism being administered truly, because of the little known Roman Catholic 'Doctrine of Intention'. This is a fact *"...since the Sacrament is not formed without the intention of the minister, and no one can see the intention of another. Intention makes the priest master of the Sacraments. He can dispense or withhold grace at his will and consequently salvation. He leaves his flock in uncertainty as to whether they have ever truly been baptized, confirmed or absolved, or of ever partaking of the Lord's Supper or Extreme Unction! Nor on the same hypothesis can he be sure he is a priest himself, or the Pope truly the Pope."*[8]

Clearly, the most serious claim made by Rome in regards to baptism is that baptism is the means to justification! It is taught that original, as well as any actual sin or guilt including all punishment due to them, is forgiven at baptism. The infant is *infused* with righteousness. Not the righteousness of Christ, however, that is imputed/charged, to every true believer—the baptized infant is simply made righteous in the sight of God. The true Biblical teaching of justification by grace alone is denounced as dangerous heresy by the Roman Catholic Church, and a curse is placed upon any who believe it!

In fact, the Council of Trent placed a curse, which still remains today, upon any who hold to the Bible's teaching of justification by grace through faith in the Lord Jesus Christ: *"If anyone saith that justifying faith is nothing else but confidence in the divine mercy which remits sin for Christ's sake alone; or, that this confidence alone is that whereby we are justified, let him be anathema (accursed)."*

It is interesting to note that, in holding to this non-biblical position, the Roman Catholic Church also rejects the teachings of one of her own church fathers, **Augustine**, who strongly believed that salvation IS purely by the grace of God.

THE ORIGIN AND HISTORY OF BAPTISM

The doctrine of baptismal regeneration was originally a Babylonian concept. The idea of infant baptism is noticeably absent from any of the early Apostolic and historical writings and documents.

Mention was first made of child baptism early in the 3rd century and became common by the middle of that century. Both adult and infant baptism co-existed until the 6th century, after which time only infant baptism was practiced in the Roman Church. The two reasons for this were the high infant mortality rate and the belief that one who died unbaptized would never see God.

Infant baptism initially took place in private ceremonies, which occurred outside of church buildings. According to *The History of Christianity*: *"As early as the end of the 2nd century some people had come to believe that baptism had a MAGICAL effect. Tertullian mentions prayer to 'sanctify' the water, and from then on it was widely believed that baptism automatically washed away sins. From this period, too, there arose the practice of exorcizing the candidate before baptism, a practice often accompanied with ceremonial anointing with oil."*[9]

It is important to make special note here that the idea of baptismal regeneration is yet another doctrine presented to Roman Catholics as Christian teaching that did not originate within the Roman Catholic Church, and certainly has no connection at all with biblical Christianity. Baptismal regeneration, however, had been a familiar practice of the Hindus of India centuries before Roman Catholicism decided to continue this popular pagan tradition by adopting the practice and calling it 'Christian'. The Brahmins (priests of the Indian god Brahma), who were also believers in baptismal regeneration, *"...make it their distinguishing boast that they are 'twice-born men' (or 'the initiated') and that, as such, they are sure of eternal happiness."*[10]

Such was also the case in Babylon where the new birth was made possible (achievable) through baptism. It was noted by **Tertullian** that

"In certain sacred rites of the heathen," with particular reference to the worship of Isis and Mithra, *" the mode of initiation is by baptism."*[11]

Further to this, **Tertullian** says that those who were thus baptized, in consequence, were promised *"...regeneration and the pardon of all their perjuries."*[12] In addition, worshippers of the chief Norse god, Odin, also practiced baptismal rites. Originally, it was believed that all *"...guilt and corruption of their new-born children could be washed away by sprinkling them with water or by plunging them, as soon as they were born, into lakes or rivers."*[13]

Baptismal regeneration was also found amongst the natives of Mexico at the time of the Cortez invasion of 1532. Later, Spanish Roman Catholic missionaries watched in amazement as a baptismal ceremony was performed by the heathen of Mexico. One such ceremony was performed by a midwife who, in Mexico it seems, was considered a priestess of sorts. It is interesting to note, and far beyond a mere coincidence, that Rome also authorizes midwives to administer this sacrament! Baptism is such an essential and indispensable part of salvation in the Roman Catholic Church that all avenues must be covered to ensure an infant does not die without being baptized.

Upon sprinkling water on the infant's head, the Mexican midwife proclaimed the following: *"...O my child, take and receive the water of the Lord of the world, which is our life, which is given for the increasing and renewing of our body. IT IS*

TO WASH AND PURIFY. I pray that these heavenly drops may enter into your body, and dwell there; that they may destroy and remove from you all the evil and sin which was given you before the beginning of the world, since all of us are under its power." The woman then addressed her words to any evil presence within the child: *"Whencesoever thou comest, thou that art hurtful to this child, LEAVE HIM AND DEPART FROM HIM, for he now liveth ANEW and is BORN ANEW; now he is PURIFIED AND CLEANSED AFRESH, and our mother Chalchwitlyene (the goddess of water) bringeth him into the world."*[14]

Along with its pagan counterpart, it is notable that exorcism also plays an important role in Roman Catholic baptism. The Devil is presumably cast out of the infant by the priest who commands, *"Depart from him, thou unclean spirit, and give place to the Holy Ghost the Comforter."*[15] Let it be stated that nowhere in the Roman Catholic New Testament is exorcism performed on the one being baptized before, during or after true Christian baptism. This practice is thoroughly pagan and therefore an abomination in the sight of God.

We see then in this pagan Mexican ceremony the same baptismal regeneration as practiced by the Roman Catholic Church to this day! The origins of Mexican mythology, including the doctrine of baptismal regeneration, which was also held by the Egyptian and Persian worshippers of the Chaldean Queen of Heaven, may be traced back to Chaldea. *"This...is a very striking proof, at once of the unity of the human race, and of the widespread diffusion of the false and abominable religious system that began at Babel."[16]* **That abominable religious system is thriving today under the guise of Roman Catholicism.**

As part of the Babylonian Mysteries, we find intermingled with the worship of the Queen of Heaven and her son a commemoration of the Flood, the Ark and other major events in the life of Noah. *"Noah, as having lived in two worlds, both before the flood and after it, was called 'Diphueis' or 'twice-born', and was represented as a god with two heads looking in opposite directions..."[17]*

The Chaldeans believed that if they were to pass through the baptismal waters, they would be made like unto 'Diphueis', 'twice-born' or 'regenerated'. This, it was believed, would entitle them to all the privileges of 'righteous' Noah and grant to them that 'new birth', which they were convinced was a fundamental ingredient in achieving eternal happiness. *"The papacy acts on precisely the same principle; and from this very source has its doctrine of baptismal regeneration been derived...."[18]*

<u>LEARN NOT THE CUSTOMS OF THE NATIONS!!</u>

We have thus far determined, from various historical accounts, the altogether pagan origin of baptismal regeneration and infant baptism. That these concepts are in fact non-biblical is readily admitted to by various leaders of the Roman Catholic Church.

We find the following words of the 'learned divine' **Jodocus Tiletanus** of Louraine striking: *"For we do bless the water wherewith we baptize, and the oil wherewith we anoint; yea, and besides that, him that is christened. And (I pray you) out of what Scripture have we learned the same? Have we it not of a SECRET AND UNWRITTEN ORDINANCE? ....Yea, I pray you, whence cometh it, that we do dip the child three times in the water? Doth it not come out of this hidden and undisclosed doctrine, which our forefathers have received closely without any curiosity, and do observe it still."*[19]

This statement clearly demonstrates that the concept of infant baptism came not from the pages of the Bible but from *secret and unwritten ordinances*. It is of vital importance for all Roman Catholics to take note at this point, that it is for you to decide whether you are going to continue to put your trust and eternal future in the doctrines of mere men, **which have no Scriptural basis,** or in the truth of the proven, reliable and infallible Word of God. Perhaps the following quite shocking revelation will help you decide: Roman Catholic Cardinal, **John Henry Newman**, conceded the fact that 'holy water' and many other things used by the Church of Rome were *"...the very instruments and appendages of demon-worship..."* And that they were ALL of *"...pagan origin"* and *"...sanctified by adoption into the Church* (of Rome).*"*[20]

In the same document, Cardinal **Newman** reconciles the Roman Catholic Church's usage of pagan-demonic worship methods and doctrines with the fact that Rome had *"...confidence in the power of Christianity to resist the infection of evil"* and to convert them to *"...an evangelical use."*

Now, this view may be accompanied by a deep sincerity, but serving and worshipping the true God with old pagan methods is abomination to God and is utterly condemned in the pages of the Roman Catholic Bible. In fact, in complete contrast with the above statements made by Cardinal **Newman**, the official footnotes to 2 Corinthians 6:14-16a in the Roman Catholic Bible state quite simply: *"...CHRISTIANITY IS NOT COMPATIBLE WITH PAGANISM."* **How then can the Roman Catholic Church ever justify, in all good conscience before her people, its blatant use of pagan/demonic methods of worship?** This is a question that all Roman Catholics should think about and work through if they take the matter of right belief in the one, true God seriously.

The nation of Israel displeased God by following the heathen nations and mingling the pagan's manner of worship with their own. **This is but one of many biblical precedents of God's hatred for all things pagan.** 2 Kings 17:15 records for us the fact that Israel ***"...followed the surrounding nations WHOM THE LORD HAD COMMANDED THEM NOT TO IMITATE."*** In Jeremiah 10:2 we see God's warning to His people: ***"Thus saith the Lord, 'LEARN NOT THE CUSTOMS OF THE NATIONS...'"***

In light of the evidence that we have presented, it is true to say that infant baptism and baptismal regeneration qualify as part of the 'customs of the nations', as Scripture calls them—the nations being any and all people who were not the people of God—and should not be, and are not, practiced by the true Christian. However much they may be accompanied by sincerity to worship and please the true God, they can never do so. Nadab and Abihu, the sons of Aaron, the first high priest of Israel, and priests themselves, are a prime example: ***"...they offered up before the Lord profane fire, such as <u>He had not authorized</u>. Fire therefore came forth from the Lord's presence and consumed them, so that they died in His presence"*** (Leviticus 10:1,2). God Himself has commanded His people, in relation to the pagan way of worship, ***"YOU SHALL NOT THUS WORSHIP THE LORD YOUR GOD"*** (Deuteronomy 12:31).

<u>WHAT DOES THE ROMAN CATHOLIC BIBLE SAY?</u>

Nowhere can it be found in the pages of the Roman Catholic Bible that true Christian regeneration is received in the sacrament of baptism. Neither can the notion of infant baptism find any support in the pages of the Roman Catholic Bible, for it clearly demonstrates that baptism **ALWAYS FOLLOWS BELIEF!!** In other words, no one in the New Testament ever received the true Christian baptism who was not first a believer of the one and only Gospel of God.

True Christian baptism finds its roots in Judaism, and is a 'public washing' that identifies the believer with the Death and Resurrection of the Lord Jesus Christ. It is a purely symbolical and outward act of what has occurred within the believer at the point of his conversion.

Biblical baptism is the symbol of regeneration through union with Christ, through faith by the grace/gift of God. **No one is saved by it and none are lost without it.** In addition, Jesus' commandment in Matthew 28:19 indicates that it was the disciples of Christ who were to be baptized and not infants. Jesus Christ said: ***"Go, therefore, and make DISCIPLES of all nations, baptizing THEM in the name of the Father, and of the Son, and of the Holy Spirit."***

The apostle Peter's address to the Jews in Acts 2 included his instructions for them to ***"...Repent and be baptized..."*** (v.38). Later, in v.41, we see that ***"Those who accepted his message were baptized..."*** Acts 8:12 sheds further light on the matter: ***"but once they BEGAN TO BELIEVE...men and women alike were baptized."*** And Acts 18:8 says, ***"...many of the Corinthians who heard BELIEVED and were baptized."*** John 3:18 states: ***"Whosoever BELIEVES in Him will not be condemned..."***.

Verse 36 of the same chapter says, ***"Whosoever BELIEVES in the Son has eternal life..."***

In all of these Scriptures, straight out of the Roman Catholic Bible, it is evident that those who were baptized were people who believed the truth of Jesus PRIOR TO THEIR BAPTISM!! *"Since it is intended only for the regenerate, baptism can never be the MEANS of regeneration. It is the appointed SIGN, but never the CONDITION of forgiveness of sins."*[21]

Also pertinent to our study is the fact that the Old Testament saints were not baptized in order to be saved or regenerated. They went to heaven by reason of their faith in the coming Messiah. We see this in Romans 4:3: ***"...Abraham BELIEVED God, and it was credited to him as RIGHTEOUSNESS."*** Righteousness came not by any ceremonial sprinkling of water, not even by circumcision, but by God-given faith in Christ.

The same is true for the Christian today. True Biblical baptism is a public confession that one is ALREADY a believer in Jesus Christ; that one is ALREADY saved, and, that one has ALREADY received the Holy Spirit.

The following Scripture is a case in point: ***"Can anyone withhold the water for baptizing these people, who HAVE received the Holy Spirit even as we have?"*** (Acts 10:47). Is it any wonder that there is nothing in the footnotes to this verse in the Roman Catholic Bible. BAPTISM, dear Roman Catholic, DOES NOT SAVE ANYONE!

Only faith in the Lord Jesus Christ can save a person. Jesus said: ***"...no one comes to the Father but by Me"*** (John 14:6). **Please note also that Jesus Christ was not baptized as an infant, but as an adult by John the Baptist.** This particular baptism was a fulfilling of the Mosaic law which required all priests to be consecrated at approximately 30 years of age (see Numbers 4:3; Exodus 29:4-7; Leviticus 8:6-36).

The fact that baptism does not regenerate or save anybody is also evident in the case of Simon Magus, recorded for us in Acts 8. Simon was a magician, who, after hearing Phillip, believed and was baptized (see v.13). However, Peter was later to declare Simon to be ***"...filled with bitter gall and...in the bonds of iniquity"*** v.23 (see also vv.20-22). *"The doctrine of Rome, however, is that all who are canonically baptized, however ignorant, however immoral, if they only give implicit faith to the (Roman Catholic) Church, and surrender their conscience to the priests, are as much regenerated as ever they can be..."*[22]

And yet, as we have just seen, according to the Roman Catholic Bible, faith in Christ was required BEFORE anyone could be baptized. All others were refused the ordinance.

Baptism is to the New Testament what circumcision was to the Old Testament, in terms of it being a visual seal of the new birth. It did not in any way bring about that new birth but was a symbol of it. Romans 4:11 says of Abraham: ***"...he received the sign of circumcision as a SEAL of the righteousness received***

THROUGH FAITH while he was UNCIRCUMCISED..." Circumcision did not MAKE Abraham righteous anymore than baptism makes a person righteous. As we see in Romans 4:9,10, Abraham's righteousness was received through faith BEFORE he was circumcised. The rite of circumcision merely declared him righteous, it was a seal of that righteousness. So too, baptism in the New Testament is always performed on a person who IS A BELIEVER. One who has ALREADY been made righteous through faith in Jesus Christ. Baptism is a *seal* of righteousness already charged to the believer and not the *cause*.

"As circumcision was the sign and seal of the Abrahamic Covenant and practiced under the Mosaic Covenant, so baptism is construed as the sign and seal of the New Covenant of the Gospel. Baptism, under the new economy, takes the place of circumcision under the old (see Colossians 2:10-12)."[23]

The key Scripture upon which the Roman Catholic doctrine of baptism rests is John 3:5: ***"Jesus answered, 'Amen, amen, I say to you, no one can enter the kingdom of God without being born of water and Spirit.'"*** Roman Catholics, when studying this verse, need to be sure that they read the entire third chapter of John's Gospel and not just this one verse alone. One must always read the Holy Scriptures of God in their proper context, or risk perverting its true meaning.

It is Rome's contention that the 'water' mentioned in this verse is a reference to baptism.

However, we learn from other passages in John's Gospel that water is used symbolically of the Word of God. For instance, Jesus says to God the Father in John 17:17: ***"Consecrate them in the truth. Your Word is truth."*** The word *consecrate* here means *to render clean*. In John 15:3 Jesus says, ***"You are already pruned because of the Word that I spoke to you."*** The word translated *pruned* here also carries with it the meaning *clean, clear, pure.* This 'cleansing' is done by the Word of God.

Returning to John 3:5 where Jesus said ***"...no one can enter the Kingdom of God without being born of water and Spirit",*** it is true to say that the term *"'born of water and of the Spirit' means that a person must be born-again by the Holy Spirit using the Scripture. It is of a surety that no one could be born-again without the Word of God applied by the Spirit of God. One today is born from above by the use of water, which is the Word of God, and the Spirit, the Holy Spirit, making it real to the heart."*[24]

Perhaps the verse which speaks with clearest distinction in associating the Word of God with water—a cleansing agent—is Ephesians 5:26, which says: ***"to sanctify her*** (the Church) ***CLEANSING HER BY THE BATH OF WATER WITH THE WORD"*** (c.f. 1 Peter 1:22). *"God's method seems to be the Word of God, used by the Spirit of God, given through a man of God. One can be confident that our Lord, saying that one must be born of water and of the Spirit, was* *referring to the Spirit of God using the Word of God.*"[25]

If baptism is such an integral part of salvation, as the Roman Catholic Church would have us believe, the thinking Roman Catholic must ask himself the question: 'Why then do so many Scriptures, when dealing with salvation, not even mention it?'

Here are even more convincing examples of Scriptures which connect cleansing and being born-again with the Word of God: ***"You have been born anew, not from perishable but from imperishable seed, through the living and abiding Word of God"*** (1 Peter 1:23). Not through Baptism!! Even the Roman Catholic footnotes to this verse contain no mention of baptism, but clearly state that *"The new birth of Christians derives from Christ..."* In Acts 2:21 we read: ***"And it shall be that everyone shall be saved who calls on the name of the Lord."*** Again, no mention of water baptism. Additionally, we must not fail to point out that the sins of a true Christian are washed away by the blood of Christ, not by the waters of baptism!

The jailer in Acts 16 asked the apostle Paul and Silas, ***"...sirs, what must I do to be saved?"*** (v.30). Paul and Silas promptly answered, ***"...BELIEVE in the Lord Jesus and you and your household will be saved."*** According to Acts 16, the jailer was taught the Gospel of Christ. By God's grace, the jailer and his household did believe and they were THEN baptized (v.33) AFTER they had believed the Gospel.

Baptism does not, indeed cannot, save you, for it was never intended to by God. Romans 3:24 speaks clearly of what DOES save us. We *"...are justified freely by HIS GRACE through the redemption IN CHRIST JESUS",* not by the waters of baptism. The one who is saved is the one who believes the Gospel of Jesus Christ, not the different gospel of Roman Catholicism.

"Those who believe the Gospel should then be baptized, not in order to MAKE them true believers, but because they have already been MADE true believers through personal faith in Jesus Christ (see Matthew 28:19)."[26]

COME OUT FROM HER....

The purpose of this booklet has not been to judge or condemn you, the Roman Catholic, but has been designed to educate you, to inform you of facts and proper biblical teaching which the Roman Catholic Church has not given you. It has been written in order to provide you with historical facts about the origins of many of your Church's teachings and traditions. **You have read for yourself what the Roman Catholic Church admits to and what your own Roman Catholic Bible says, and doesn't say—what it teaches and simply does not support.** Ultimately, this booklet is a plea for you to come out of the Roman Catholic Church, away from all its man-made doctrines and pagan practices, away from its false gospel. **God must be worshipped HIS way, for no other way is acceptable unto Him.** There is no other way to worship the true God—**and therefore be a saved, justified and true follower of God**—other than the way He has prescribed in His Holy Word. **There is no Gospel that must be believed, by which a man is saved, other than the one that reveals the Righteousness of Christ.**

We have presented the truth to you. **Verifiable truth.** We have quoted from many sources approved by your own Church including a Church approved Bible. But do not believe things simply because you saw them written in a booklet. The Bible commends those who properly investigate what is presented to them as truth and we encourage you to do so. In Acts 17:11 the apostle Paul and Silas preached to the people at Berea. The Roman Catholic Bible says that ***"These...were more fair-minded than those in Thessalonica, for they received the word with all willingness and EXAMINED THE SCRIPTURES DAILY TO DETERMINE WHETHER THESE THINGS WERE SO."*** The Scriptures were their sole authority. They did not refer to the writings of mere men, seeking out their opinions, but went immediately to the Holy Word of God **knowing** that His Word alone could be trusted, and was the sure test for all teachings being presented as God's own decrees (see 2 Peter 1:19). Paul and Silas were not offended by their examining and putting to the test what they was saying, they did not say *'How dare you* *examine what we have said to you; don't you know who we are?'* **Every Christian, indeed every person, is to examine by the Holy Scriptures all that is presented to him as God's teaching, and if it does not match with the Scriptures, you can be sure it did not come from God and is to be rejected out of hand.** Writing to true believers, John said, ***"Beloved, DO NOT TRUST every spirit BUT TEST the spirits to see whether they belong to God, because many false prophets have gone out into the world"*** (1 John 4:1).

The subtle deceptiveness of the Roman Catholic Church is that she teaches some truths of Scripture but always adds to them, something which the Scriptures roundly condemn: ***"Add NOTHING to HIS Words, lest He reprove you, and you be exposed as a deceiver"*** (Proverbs 30:6). In speaking against such deception the Lord Jesus warned His disciples to ***"...Look out, and beware of the leaven of the Pharisees and Sadducees"*** (Matthew 16:6 cf. Galatians 5:9). Later, the disciples ***"...understood that He was not telling them to beware of the leaven of bread, but of THE TEACHING of the Pharisees and Sadducees"*** (Matthew 16:12). The Pharisees and Sadducees were the religious leaders in Jesus' day. The apostle Paul warned: ***"...watch out for those who create dissensions and obstacles, in opposition to the teaching that you learned; avoid them. For such people do not serve our Lord Christ but their own appetites, and by fair and***

flattering speech they deceive the hearts of the innocent" (Romans 16:17,18). EXAMINE EVERYTHING! TEST EVERYTHING BY THE WORD OF GOD! **For we are dealing with eternal issues here. We are dealing with heaven and hell, and what a person believes determines their eternal destiny, for the doctrine you hold to is the surest evidence of whether or not it is the true God Who has revealed Himself to you or whether it is a false god whom you have embraced.**

Some examples of such deceptiveness are as follows: the Roman Catholic Church teaches her followers to pray the Lord's prayer, but they are encouraged to do so whilst holding the Rosary which is a pagan invention and has nothing to do with true Christianity. Yes, Rome agrees that God alone forgives sin, but they add that this power to forgive has been given to her priests and one must go *to them* to receive it and not directly to God the Father through Jesus His Son, as the Scriptures prescribe. Yes, Roman Catholicism teaches that the Bible is the Word of God but it considers tradition to be *equal* to God's precious Holy Word and insists that she is the only true interpreter of Scripture! **In other words, what ROME says God's Word is saying is what is to be obeyed, rather than what the Scripture's interpretation of Itself is saying! Compare Scripture with Scripture, not Scripture with a man's interpretation.** All along, Roman Catholicism adds to God's Word and in other instances withholds certain parts of it, such as the second Commandment, from its publications. It is true that Roman Catholicism teaches 'the death, burial and resurrection' of Jesus Christ but it is vitally important to note that while she may correctly teach some aspects of these things—things which are aligned with historical fact—the Roman Catholic Church **does not** teach the death, burial and resurrection of Jesus Christ ***"...in accordance with the Scriptures..."*** (1 Corinthians 15:3,4).

It is no accident that so much pagan tradition is found today in Roman Catholicism. It has been carefully managed and seen to, that old pagan/occultic rites and traditions, which the Bible calls demonic, are continued to be adhered to and promoted as vigilantly as they were by the early pagans, but now with a Christian veneer thus setting up the Roman Catholic Church as the unmistakably identifiable anti-christian system referred to as 'Babylon' in the Bible. Roman Catholicism stands today not only against Christ, for it does not teach His Gospel, but Rome has also, in a most vulgar way, usurped Christ's position. The papacy claims that **it** is the vicar of Christ on earth, rather than the Holy Spirit as the Word of God says.

That which immediately reveals a religious organization's ungodly foundation may be seen in the gospel it teaches. What a person, or organization such as the Roman Catholic Church, says about **Who Jesus Christ is, what He has done and for whom He has done it**—in other words His Person and His Work—will reveal whether or not that person or organization is of God (see 2 John 9). After having preached to them the True and only Gospel of salvation which reveals the true God and true Christ, Paul the apostle warned the believers in Galatia that ***"...even if we or an angel from heaven should preach to you a gospel OTHER THAN the one that we preached to you, let that one be accursed"*** (Galatians 1:8).

There are many who by nature are religious; many who are extremely zealous for what they believe to be the things of God, yet Scripture reminds us that by nature ***"There is no one just, not one, there is no one who understands, there is no one who seeks God"*** (Romans 3:10,11). Saving, God-given faith in the true and only Gospel of God shows that it is the true God Who has revealed Himself. **Belief in any gospel other than that one and only Gospel of God reveals that it is not the true God Who has revealed Himself but rather a false god who cannot save.**

We implore you to come out of the Roman Catholic Church. A Church which is headed, not by the Lord Jesus Christ, for it does not promote His Gospel, but by a man who calls himself the 'Pope', and who allows himself to be addressed as 'Holy Father', a title which God **ALONE** is worthy. God ALONE is Father, and God ALONE is Holy. The Lord Jesus only ever referred to God as 'Father', and in Revelation 15:4 Jesus, praying to the Father said: ***"...You ALONE are Holy..."*** How dare ANY man take upon himself a title of which ONLY God is worthy! Not incidentally, the Lord Jesus Christ also said to His followers not to call any man on earth father, that is in a spiritual sense, for One was their Father and He resides in heaven: ***"Call no one on earth your father; you have but one Father in heaven"*** (Matthew 23:9). Roman Catholicism responds to these words of the Lord Jesus by calling *every one of its priests 'father'*, and demanding that everyone else, Roman Catholic or not, do likewise despite admitting in their footnotes to Matthew 23:9 that, *"...Jesus forbids not only the titles (rabbi, father and master) but the spirit of superiority and pride that is shown by their acceptance."*

Pope Leo XIII once blasphemously declared: *"The Pope holds upon this earth the place of God Almighty..."* **Robert Bellermine**, famous Jesuit Cardinal of the 16th century and also a saint of the Roman Catholic Church, had this to say: *"All the names which in the Scriptures are applied to Christ by virtue of which it is established that He is over the Church, all the same names are applied to the Pope."* The *Catholique Nationale* of Paris, in its July 13, 1895 issue, contained the following claim made by the then archbishop of Venice, later to become Pope Pius X. He said, *"The Pope is not only the representative of Jesus Christ, but he is Jesus Christ Himself hidden under the veil of the flesh..."* Dear Roman Catholic, **the Pope is NOT Jesus Christ! JESUS CHRIST IS GOD!! ONLY through the Lord Jesus Christ is there**

salvation, not through the Pope and his 'church' of Rome.

"History is replete with sayings that mocked Romanism's false claim to celibacy: 'The holiest hermit has his whore'" and *"'Rome has more prostitutes than any other city because she has the most celibates'"* are examples. Pope Pius II called Rome *'The only city run by bastards, the sons and grandsons of popes and cardinals'.*

"Even Roman Catholic historians admit that among the popes were some of the most degenerate and unconscionable ogres in all history. More than one pope was slain by a husband who found him in bed with his wife. To call such a man 'His holiness vicar of Christ' makes a mockery of holiness and Christ. Yet the name of each of these mass murderers, fornicators, robbers, warmongers—some guilty of the massacre of thousands—is emblazoned in honor on the Church's official list of Peter's alleged successors, the popes" ('The Berean Call', July '94, p.2).

"Will you believe the words of the Roman Catholic Church or will you believe the words of the Roman Catholic Bible? It is for you to decide. Remember, there are only two religions in the entire world, man's and God's. If it is not the truth of God that you are believing, then you have embraced the lies of the Devil." **You have embraced a false gospel wherein is no salvation.** *"Man's religion is by works—his own efforts, his fastings and prayers, his obedience to the Church. That, in effect, makes him his own*

saviour. God's is by faith in the finished work of Jesus Christ. Jesus paid it all... The Roman Catholic Bible states clearly: **"...we have been JUSTIFIED BY FAITH, we have peace with God through our Lord Jesus Christ...***Romans 5:1."* *The Roman Catholic Bible makes it perfectly clear that man cannot save himself and that Christ is his only hope; his only Saviour."*[27]

"Salvation is not dependent on a human priest, Mary, Baptism, the saints, the sacraments, the Mass, confession, good works, membership in the Roman Catholic Church or the Pope."

Salvation is not gained by our loyalty or service to a person—**be they our parents or grandparents and their religious traditions which they have passed down to us**—or to an institution such as the Roman Catholic Church, but rather by our **acceptance of the truth**!! *"Jesus said:* **"...I am the Way and the Truth and the Life. No one comes to the Father EXCEPT THROUGH ME"** *(John 14:6)* and **"I am the Gate. Whoever enters through Me will be saved..."** (John 10:9). *Acts 4:12 says:* **'There is NO salvation through ANYONE else, nor is there ANY other name under heaven given to the human race by which we are to be saved.'**

It matters not how religious a person is or how sincere he might be in his religious pursuits, if a man has not the Gospel of God, if he does not **"...remain in the teaching of the Christ** (he) **does not have God..."** (2 John 9). **"That all who have not believed the truth but have approved wrongdoing may be condemned"**

(2 Thessalonians 2:12). Scripture also speaks of the vengeance that will be had upon the enemies of God *"...at the revelation of the Lord Jesus from heaven with His mighty angels, in blazing fire, inflicting punishment on those who do not acknowledge God and on those WHO DO NOT OBEY THE GOSPEL of our Lord Jesus. These will pay the penalty of eternal ruin, separated from the presence of the Lord and from the glory of His power"* (1 Thessalonians 7-9).

Only through the Gospel of Christ wherein is revealed the Righteousness of Christ, without which no man can be saved, is there true salvation: *"For I am not ashamed of the Gospel. IT IS THE POWER OF GOD for the salvation of everyone who believes: for the Jew first, and then Greek. For in it is revealed the Righteousness of God from faith to faith; as it is written, the one who is righteous <u>by faith</u> will live"* (Romans 1:16,17). Central to the Gospel message is the Person and Work of Jesus Christ and, according to the Scriptures, if one is wrong about Christ, if one has embraced erroneous doctrine concerning Christ the Person and His Work, one is not merely in need of correction yet nevertheless saved, one has in fact fallen for another jesus who is identified by false doctrine, and thus remains in a lost state. **Only in the True Jesus is their salvation. Belief, however sincere, in a false jesus CANNOT SAVE!** You see, not only does the apostle Paul state that the Gospel is the power of God but he also defines this statement in 1 Corinthians 1:18: *"THE MESSAGE OF THE CROSS is foolishness to those who are perishing, but to us who are being saved IT* (THE CROSS) *IS THE POWER OF GOD."*

Belief in false doctrines concerning Christ constitutes a belief in *another* gospel, one which does not represent the true Christ but a false savior (see 2 Corinthians 11:3,4). The Holy Spirit is the Spirit of Truth (John 14:17; 15:26; 16:13) and never presents a man with, nor leads him to believe, a false gospel: *"But when He comes, the Spirit of Truth, He will guide you to all truth..."* (John 16:13). Jesus prayed, *"Consecrate them in the Truth. Your Word is Truth"* (John 17:17). The true believer is consecrated, or sanctified, through the truth which is the Word of God and not through the lies of men. Speaking to saved men, the apostle Paul stated: *"...God chose you as the firstfruits for salvation through sanctification BY THE SPIRIT <u>AND</u> BELIEF IN TRUTH"* (2 Thessalonians 2:13). There is no true sanctification if one's faith is not in the Truth of God.

Only by belief in Christ's Gospel, which says that man is dead in sin, without God and without hope of salvation by anything he is or does in an effort to please God and gain His favor, is a man saved: *"Therefore, remember that at one time you...were at that time without Christ...without hope and without God in the world"* (Ephesians 2:11-13). *"You were dead in* *your transgressions and sins"* (Ephesians 2:1). ***"All have sinned and are deprived of the glory of God"*** (Romans 3:23).

Only by belief in Christ's Gospel, which says that a man is saved not by works, not by anything he has done, is doing or will do, but solely by the grace and mercy of God, is a man saved: ***"...a person is not justified by works of the law but through faith in Jesus Christ, even we have believed in Christ Jesus that we may be justified by faith in Christ and not by works of the law, because by works of the law no one will be justified"*** (Galatians 1:16). The cry of the truly justified sinner is that he is ***"...justified freely by His grace through the redemption in Christ Jesus, Whom God set forth as an expiation, through faith, by His blood..."*** (Romans 3:24,25).

Only by belief in Christ's Gospel, which says a man is not saved based on anything he has done but solely by the grace of God through the election of grace, is a man saved: ***"...God chose you as the firstfruits for salvation through sanctification by the Spirit and belief in truth"*** (2 Thessalonians 2:13). ***"As He chose us in Him, before the foundation of the world, to be holy and without blemish before Him"*** (Ephesians 1:4); ***"He saved us and called us to a holy life, NOT ACCORDING TO OUR WORKS, but according to His own design and the grace bestowed on us in Christ Jesus before time began"*** (2 Timothy 1:9). No saved person ever came to God first (see 1 John 4:19). In every case God came to the person first and gave them the gift of salvation, not because they had in any way earned this gift, but freely and only by the will of God and the grace of God. Scripture says that by nature **"...there is no one who seeks God"** (Romans 3:11). **"But when one does not work, yet believes in the One Who justifies the ungodly, his faith is credited as righteousness. So also David declares the blessedness of the person to whom God credits righteousness apart from works"** (Romans 4:5,6).

Only by belief in Christ's Gospel, which says that Christ died exclusively for His people, those whom God had given Him (see John 17:2), and has provided them with an atonement for their sin, having their sins imputed, or charged, to Him and imputing unto them His perfect righteousness, is a man saved. Jesus said: **"I am the good shepherd. A good shepherd lays down His life for the sheep....I will lay down My life for the sheep"** (John 10:11,15). Writing to true believers Paul said, **"For our sake He made Him to be sin** (for us) **who did not know sin, so that we might become the righteousness of God in Him"** (2 Corinthians 5:21).

Only by belief in Christ's Gospel, which says that all His people shall come to Him, hear and believe His Gospel, is there true salvation. None whom the Lord has given unto Him shall perish, none shall be plucked from His Hand, but all for whom He died shall be saved: **"My sheep**

__hear My voice; I know them, and they follow Me. I give them eternal life, and they shall never perish. No one can take them out of My hand"__ (John 10:27,28). *__"Everything that the Father gives Me WILL come to Me..."__* (John 6:37).

__Only by belief in Christ's Gospel,__ which states that none for whom He died shall ever perish, but all who have had their sins charged to Him shall be given eternal life, is a man saved. Salvation has not only been *obtained* for God's chosen, but it is eternally *maintained* by the Will of God and all that Christ has done: *__"...Give glory to Your Son, so that Your Son may glorify You, just as You gave Him authority over all people, so that He may give eternal life to all You gave Him"__* (John 17:1,2). Christ has not only obtained salvation for His people, by paying the penalty for their sin and imputing to them His righteousness, He also maintains their salvation by His eternal and completed work upon the cross. Thus ALL the glory for salvation belongs to God and none of it is shared with any man based on his works. __Only THIS Gospel gives ALL the glory to God for salvation and wherein there is no room for man to boast in anything he is or has done.__

__Only by belief in Christ's Gospel,__ which states that no man is, or can be saved by his own righteousness, by his own efforts at obedience to God's Law, but only by the perfect Righteousness of Jesus Christ which is freely imputed based on His grace and mercy ALONE to all those for whom

He died, is a man saved. The apostle Paul wanted to ***"...be found in Him, not having any righteousness of my own based on the law but that which comes through faith in Christ, the righteousness from God, depending on faith..."*** (Philippians 3:9). Paul considered all that he was and did in the realm of religion as rubbish, **and therefore himself as a lost person,** before knowing Christ and His Gospel: ***"...because of the supreme good of knowing Christ Jesus my Lord. For His sake I have accepted the loss of all things and I consider them so much rubbish..."*** (Philippians 3:8).

Only those who have heard the Word of Truth, God's Mighty Gospel, can be said to truly hope in the true Christ: ***"In Him you also, who have heard the word of truth, THE GOSPEL OF YOUR SALVATION, and have believed in Him, were sealed with the promised Holy Spirit"*** (Ephesians 1:13).

Look then to the only true Jesus Who is the Author and Finisher of the Faith which God gives and which only believes in the true Gospel.

ANY AND ALL FAITH IN ANOTHER JESUS WILL NOT SAVE.

ANY AND ALL FAITH IN ANOTHER GOSPEL WILL NOT SAVE.

"Whoever believes (THE Gospel) *and is baptized will be saved; whoever does not believe will be condemned"* (Mark 16:16).

The true born again believer knows that *"...by grace you have been saved through faith, and this is not from you; it is the gift of God; it is not from works, so no one may boast"* (Ephesians 2:8,9).

May God bless each and every one of you with His Truth as revealed in His Gospel.

<u>NOTES</u>

---

[1] Roman Catholic Catechism, p.41, 1937, Australian Catholic Truth Society.

[2] Ibid., p.41.

[3] The Documents of Vatican II, Abbott-Gallagher: 1966 Edit.

[4] Sincere Christian, Vol.1, p.363.

[5] Roman Catholic Catechism, op.cit., p.42.

[6] Roman Catholicism, L. Boettner, p.190, 1962, Presbyterian and Reformed Publishing Company.

[7] Roman Catholicism, (booklet), p.10, Wesley Press.

[8] Concise Guide to Bible Christianity and Romanism, 1991, p.26.

[9] The History of Christianity, organizing editor Dr. T. Dowley, p.10, 1977, Lion Publishing.

[10] The Two Babylons, Alexander Hislop, p.132, 1916, S.W. Partridge & Co.

[11] De Baptismo, Tertullian, Vol.1, p.1204.

[12] Ibid., p.1205.

[13] Hislop, op.cit., p.132.

[14] Prescott's Mexico, Vol.3, pp.339,340.

[15] Sincere Christian, Vol.1., p.365.

[16] Hislop, op.cit., p.134.

[17] Ibid., p.134.

[18] Ibid., p.137.

[19] Review of Epistle of Dr. Gentianus Harvet., p.19b, 20a.

[20] Newman's Development, pp.359, 360.

[21] New Unger's Bible Dictionary, M.F. Unger, p.143, 1988.

[22] Hislop, op.cit., p.132.

[23] Unger's Dictionary, op.cit., p.143.

[24] John, Vol.1, J.V. McGee, p.54, 1976, Thru The Bible Books.

[25] Ibid., p.54.

[26] Evangelical Catholics, S. Mawhinney, p.10, 1992, Christian Ministries Incorporated.

[27] The Catholic Bible Has The Answer , O.J. Smith.

Please Contact:

morenodalbello@yahoo.com.au

Please Visit:

www.godsonlygospel.com

Made in the USA
Monee, IL
07 July 2026

56550169R00022